Bucharest Travel Highlights

Best Attractions & Experiences

Todd MacIntyre

This publication may not be reproduced, stored in a retrieval system, or transmitted, in any form or by any means without the prior written permission of the publisher. It may not be otherwise circulated in any form of binding or cover other than that in which it is published and without similar condition being imposed on the subsequent purchaser. If there are inaccuracies in copyright acknowledgements the publisher will be pleased to insert the appropriate acknowledgement in subsequent printings of this publication. Although we have taken all reasonable care in researching this book we make no warranty about the accuracy or completeness of its content and disclaim all liability arising from its use.

Copyright © 2022, Astute Press
All Rights Reserved.

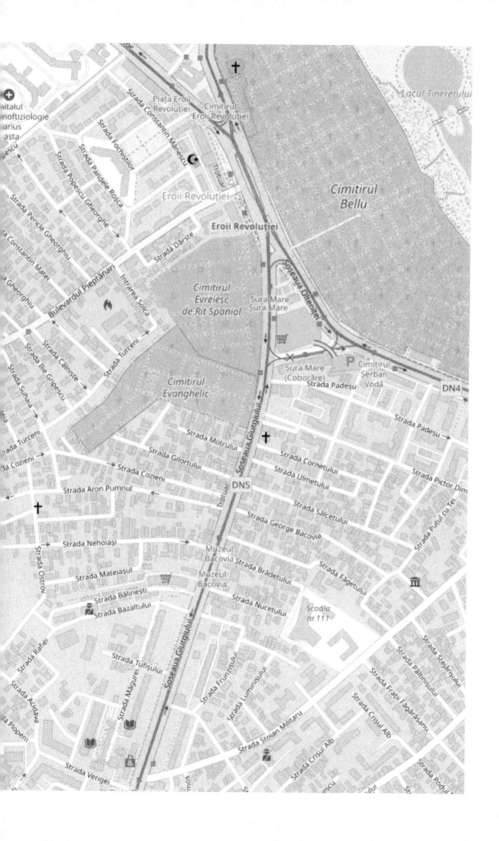

Contents

	Page
Welcome to Bucharest	7
☐ 1. Stavropoleos Church	7
☐ 2. Romanian Athenaeum	8
☐ 3. Romanian Patriarchal Cathedral	9
☐ 4. The Old Court/Princely Palace	10
☐ 5. Antim Monastery	11
☐ 6. Saint Spyridon the New Church	12
☐ 7. Cișmigiu Gardens	12
☐ 8. Calea Victoriei	13
☐ 9. University Square	15
☐ 10. Palace of the National Military Circle	15
☐ 11. Lipscani Street	16
☐ 12. Kretzulescu Church	17
☐ 13. National History Museum of Romania	18
☐ 14. National Museum of Art of Romania	19
☐ 15. Armenian Church	20
☐ 16. Dimitrie Gusti National Village Museum	21
☐ 17. Carol Park	23
☐ 18. Youth's Park	24
☐ 19. Revolution Memorial	24
☐ 20. Unirea Shopping Center	25
☐ 21. Capitoline Wolf of Bucharest	26

Bucharest Travel Highlights

☐ 22. Prince Radu Vodă Monastery 26
☐ 23. Royal Palace 27
☐ 24. Cotroceni Palace 28
☐ 25. Lake Cișmigiu 30
☐ 27. University Library 31
☐ 28. Old Princely Court Church 31
☐ 29. "I.L. Caragiale" National Theatre Museum 32
☐ 30. București Mall 33
☐ 31. Stavropoleos Monastery 34
☐ 32. National Museum of the Romanian Peasant . . . 35
☐ 33. Amzei Market 36
☐ 34. History Museum of the Romanian Jews 36
☐ 35. Church of Bucur the Shepherd 37
☐ 36. Odeon Theatre 38
☐ 37. "Theodor Pallady" Museum 39
☐ 38. Art Collections Museum 40
☐ 39. Kid's Town 41
☐ 40. National Opera House Museum 42
☐ 41. Bulevardul Unirii 42
☐ 42. Țăndărică Puppet Theatre 42
☐ 43. Church of the Icon 43
Picture Credits 43

Welcome to Bucharest

Bucharest's capital and largest city, has a bustling old quarter, impressive buildings from the time of Ceaucescu and great cafes and nightlife. Its centre is dominated by the enormous Palatul Parlamentului government building (Palace of Parliament) that looks like an enormous spaceship on its side, and the lovely leafy Cismigiu Gardens. Outside the centre, Bucharest has some fantastic museums and galleries.

Founded in 1459—making it one of Europe's oldest capitals—Bucharest is also home to Romania's largest square, Piaţa Unirii, where much of the country's history has played out.

☐ 1. Stavropoleos Church

Phone: +4021 313 4747
Web: http://www.stavropoleos.ro/

The Monastery of the Archangels Michael and Gabriel, better known as the Stavropoleos Church, was founded at the beginning of 1816 by an abbess from the monastery of Chamberia. She had two ambitious goals: to revive monastic life in Romania and introduce western European music. Her ability to attract musical talent and allow musical creativity was impressive and attracted the interest of many outstanding composers including Costanzo Anticoli, Nicolae Blaremberg and Dimitrie Poliviene.

☐ 2. Romanian Athenaeum

Address: Strada Constantin Esarcu, Bucharest, Romania
Phone: +40 21 315 2567
Web: https://www.fge.org.ro/

The Athenaeum is a landmark of the Romanian capital city, since it occupies a dominating position on Calea Victoriei, a major thoroughfare in the city center. The elaborate stone building was finished in 1888 and for more than a century it has been a place where the best of Romania's classical musicians have shown their talents. The concert hall hosts one of the most prestigious classical music festivals, also called 'George Enescu' Festival, which takes place every year from the beginning of October to mid-November.

☐ 3. Romanian Patriarchal Cathedral

The Romanian Patriarchal Cathedral is a large complex that includes many buildings. It is located on Dealul Mitropoliei, which translates to the 'Hill of the Metropolitan', in Bucharest. This cathedral was built between 1882 and 1886 by Alexandru Orăscu, succeeding an older church. The gothic revival style architecture of this cathedral was designed by the

French architect Albert Galleron, who also supervised its construction.

☐ 4. The Old Court/Princely Palace

Address: Strada Franceză 21-23, Bucharest, Romania
Phone: 021/314.03.75
Email: muzeucurteaveche@yahoo.com

It's name literally means "The Old Court" (from "Curte veche" - old court). The palace was built as a residence for Vlad III Dracula, the Prince of Wallachia (1456-1462) and it was also used by his son, Vlad the Impaler. The palace is part of the historic center of Bucharest which it added to the UNESCO World Heritage List in 1991.

☐ 5. Antim Monastery

Address: Strada Mitropolit Antim Ivireanul, Nr. 29, Sector 5, București, cod 040111, Romania
Phone: +40 314 178 078
Email: manastirea.antim@gmail.com
Web: http://manastireaantim.ro/?optm=acasa

Built between 1713 and 1715 by Saint Antim Ivireanu, a Metropolitan Bishop of the Wallachian Church, the Antim Monastery of Bucharest is a picturesque religious edifice built in Byzantine style. The frescoes in the church reveal that the monastery was built during the reign of Prince Radu Mihnea.

☐ 6. Saint Spyridon the New Church

Saint Spyridon the New Church in Bucharest is an architectural monument of great value, and also a very important religious edifice. It was built between 1860-1862, when Romania became an independent kingdom. It was designed by Carabet Ștefănescu, in the Gothic style. Patriarch Justinian modified the church between 1901-1909 in Byzantine fashion. The church was heavily damaged during World War II and between 1968-1975 it was rehabilitated, notably by architects Velicu Șerbănescu and Horia Maicu.

☐ 7. Cișmigiu Gardens

Phone: +40 744 630 000
Email: office@alpab.ro
Web: http://www.cismigiuparc.ro/

The Cișmigiu Gardens, located in the city center of Bucharest, are one of the most important green areas in the city. They form the oldest and largest park of the central area of Bucharest. The creation of the gardens by Alexandru Ioan Cuza was an important moment for Romanian history. They were named after Cișmigiu Lake, which later became a decorative pond once its original purpose was lost after the drainage works carried out in 1847-1856 under Prince Carol I.

☐ 8. Calea Victoriei

Web: http://www.fundatiacaleavictoriei.ro/

Calea Victoriei in Romania is a major avenue in central Bucharest. It leads from Splaiul Independenței to the north and then northwest up to Piața Victoriei, where Șoseaua Kiseleff continues north. It was named after victor Emmanuel of Italy, who would become King of Romania.

☐ 9. University Square

University Square is located in the center of Bucharest, surrounded by important buildings such as the Palace of Justice, the Romanian Athenaeum, the Bucharest National Theatre and the Intercontinental Hotel.

☐ 10. Palace of the National Military Circle

Address: Strada Constantin Mille 1, Bucharest, Romania
Phone: + 40 21 314 95 51
Email: marketing@cmn.ro
Web: http://www.cmn.ro/

The Officers' Circle Palace is also known as the Palace of the National Military Circle, and is located in Bucharest. It was built by architect Dimitrie Maimarolu using French neoclassical style. The beneficiary was the Officers' Circle of the Bucharest military garrison, which was founded in 1876. The palace was built on the site of the old Sărindar monastery.

☐ 11. Lipscani Street

Address: Strada Lipscani, Bucharest, Romania

The Lipscani district was, in the Middle Ages and the Early Modern era, the main business district of Bucharest. In the 16th century it became a place for horse market and during the 17th century it became a commercial area. The street was also known for its Turkish bazaar where traders from the Ottoman Empire would sell their goods.

☐ 12. Kretzulescu Church

Phone: +4021 410 7116

The Kretzulescu Church, built in 1722 for boyar Iordache Crețulescu, is thought to have been designed by the Italian architect Nicolae Porumbaru. Like other churches in Bucharest of the time, it is made of brick, with stone only on the exterior of the windows. It is unique in its simplicity, except for the unusual grouping of seven windows on each side.

☐ 13. National History Museum of Romania

Address: Calea Victoriei 12, 030026, Bucharest, Romania
Phone: +40213158207
Email: pr.mnir@gmail.com
Web: https://www.mnir.ro/

The National Museum of Romanian History is one of the oldest public museums in Europe, having been established in 1875. It has grown significantly over the years. The museum contains many historical artifacts from every part of the country, including jewelry, coins, weapons, paintings and statues. With a surface of over 8,000 square meters, it has 60 exhibition rooms housing valuable collections.

☐ 14. National Museum of Art of Romania

Address: Calea Victoriei 49-53, 010063 Bucharest, Romania
Phone: 021/313.30.30;021/314.81.19
Email: national.art@art.museum.ro
Web: http://www.mnar.arts.ro/

The National Museum of Art of Romania exhibits collections of medieval and modern Romanian art, as well as the international collection assembled by the Romanian royal family. The museum was reopened in 2004 following extensive restoration work, and is situated in the Royal Palace in Revolution Square, in central Bucharest. The collection includes works by Jacques-Louis David and includes 'Goya dentro del morrillo' (1822), an autotype showing Goya willingly surrendering himself into captivity inside a Spanish dungeon after the battle of Baylen.

☐ 15. Armenian Church

Address: Strada Armenească, Bucharest, Romania
Phone: +40 21 314 0208

Bucharest Travel Highlights

Built in 1695 by Didymoteihos Ciacovali, the Armenian Church of Bucharest is one of the places visited by thousands of tourists each year. The church has an unusual octagonal-shaped design and ornate paintings that depict stories about the New Testament. The internal part of the church features a wooden iconostasis and a mural depicting a hunting scene in which a man is shown to chase a stag with bow and arrow.

☐ 16. Dimitrie Gusti National Village Museum

Address: Șoseaua Kiseleff 28-30, Bucharest, 011347, Romania
Phone: +40 21 317 9068
Email: contact@muzeul-satului.ro
Web: http://www.muzeul-satului.ro/

Bucharest Travel Highlights

This enormous complex is more of an open-air museum than simply a palace. The entire 300,000 m2 space contains 262 rooms, 39 of which are currently allocated to the use of the royal family. The palace itself is famous for its opulent furnishings and decor, including 979 paintings, 1238 pieces of furniture and 1700 carpets.

☐ 17. Carol Park

The Carol I Park, also known as Parcul Libertatii (Liberty Park), is the oldest park in Bucharest and was founded by Prince Carol I when he was prince of Wallachia. It was named "Park of the People's enjoyment" or "Cismigiu Garden" and became a public park after the end of the communist regime.

☐ 18. Youth's Park

The lush gardens and colorful playgrounds of Tineretului Park make it a great place for kids. The park has a very popular lake area which features a large open-air swimming pool, a paddleboat cafe, and an event hall. Nearby you will find a bronze statue of a famous wrestler. Known as the "Monument to the Haiduci," the life-size statue symbolizes the struggles of the Haiduc who fought for freedom from Ottoman rule in the fourteen century.

☐ 19. Revolution Memorial

Address: Revolution Square, Bucharest, Romania

The Romanian Revolution Memorial commemorates the students who were shot by the army during the first days of the Revolution, at the intersection of Calea Victoriei and Lascar

Catargiu streets. The structure is composed of a central vertical mast with flanking slanted columns all erected on a large granite platform. At its top are two metal arcs that are joined at the centre to form a star shape.

☐ 20. Unirea Shopping Center

Address: Piaţa Unirii 3, District 3, Bucharest, Romania
Phone: + 40 21 303 0208
Email: office@unireashop.ro
Web: http://www.unireashop.ro/

Unirea Shopping Center is a chain of two large shopping centres, the initial one being located in Unirii Square, Bucharest, and the second in the city of Braşov. The Bucharest mall is the biggest shopping mall in Romania.

☐ 21. Capitoline Wolf of Bucharest

Roman Square is home to the famous Capitoline Wolf of Bucharest. The large wolf statue represents Romulus and Remus, the twin founders of Rome. Also known as the Capitoline Wolf, this 550 pound monument is one of the most recognized symbols of Bucharest.

☐ 22. Prince Radu Vodă Monastery

Address: Strada Radu Vodă 24, Bucharest, Romania

The Prince Radu Vodă Monastery is a late-Baroque monastery situated on the road that bears the same name, in central Bucharest. In 1699, Prince Constantin Brâncoveanu had a church built here, named after the patron saint of his wife Elisabeta (Elizabeth). It was erected to be her private church. Built by Constantin Șerban the Younger, it also became known as Elisabeta Church due to its dedication. The church's original decoration consisted of carved wooden ornaments.

☐ 23. Royal Palace

Address: Calea Victoriei 49-53, 70101 Bucharest, Romania
Phone: +40 21 313 30 30
Email: comunicare@art.museum.ro

The Royal Palace is a monumental building situated in the capital of Romania, on Calea Victoriei. The Palace in its various incarnations served as official residence for the Kings of Romania until 1947, when the communist regime was installed after Michael I of Romania's forced abdication. Currently it is home to the National Museum of Contemporary Art of Romania, and its surroundings are part of Bucharest's Royal Palace Court park complex.

☐ 24. Cotroceni Palace

Phone: +4 0213173107
Email: vizitare@muzeulcotroceni.ro
Web: http://www.muzeulcotroceni.ro/

The Cotroceni Palace (Romanian: Palatul Cotroceni) is the official residence of the President of Romania in Bucharest. It is located at Bulevardul Geniului, nr. 1, in the vicinity of the Herăstrău Park and not far from Baneasa Forest and Nicolae Bălcescu Monument. Newer buildings around it were designed by Anghel Saligny in neoclassic or art deco style, while older buildings such as the Cotroceni Greek Church were renovated to house clinics and museums.

☐ 25. Lake Cişmigiu

During winter the Cişmigiu Lake is frozen and a ice skate park is created. A popular spot amongst the locals is the pedestrian bridge that crosses over the lake. A new footpath encircles both of these parks and runs along the lake. The Cişmigiu Gardens consist of the picturesque Herăstrău Park and this inner garden, where tourists can enjoy a more intimate ambiance, with its romantic walks and flower beds, look outs and monuments.

☐ 27. University Library

The University Library in Bucharest is an enormous art deco building that is fit for royalty. The original building was completed in 1935 by French architect Charles Bridan. It was used as the central university library for students enrolled in the Faculty of Philosophy, Letters and Human Sciences.

☐ 28. Old Princely Court Church

Web: http://www.biserica-sfantul-anton.ro/

Across from the Royal Court of Constantin Brancoveanu is the Old Princely Court Church on Calea Victoriei. It was built around the half of the 16th century during the reign of Mircea the Shepherd, and it is the oldest church of this city.

☐ 29. "I.L. Caragiale" National Theatre Museum

Address: Bulevardul Nicolae Bălcescu 2, Bucharest, Romania
Phone: 0216/139.175
Email: tnbcomunicare@gmail.com

The history of the Caragiale National Museum began on December 24th, 1948, on the occasion of 120 years since the birth of the Romanian playwright and writer — Luca Caragiale. The exhibits include manuscripts, handwritten notes, personal photographs and autographs.

☐ 30. Bucureşti Mall

Address: Calea Vitan 55-59, Bucharest, Romania
Phone: + 40 21 327 6100
Email: office@anchorgrup.ro

The Bucureşti Mall is a shopping mall close to the Dudeşti and Văcăreşti neighbourhoods. It was the first shopping mall in Romania. Located on Calea Vitan approximately 1 km outside Bucharest's historic center, the four-story, 50,000 sqm. mall opened in 1999, in an old Ceauşescu-era abandoned giant food warehouse.

☐ 31. Stavropoleos Monastery

The Stavropoleos Monastery, also known as Stavropoleos Church during the last century when the monastery was dissolved, is an Eastern Orthodox monastery for nuns in central Bucharest. Its church is built in the Brâncovenesc style. The patrons of the church are St. Archangels Michael and Gabriel. The monastery's expertise includes Byzantine music and organ liturgy.

☐ 32. National Museum of the Romanian Peasant

Phone: 021/317.96.61; 021/317.96.64; 021/317.96.65
Email: <info@muzeultaranuluiroman.ro; vsnitulescu@yahoo.co.uk>
Web: http://www.muzeultaranuluiroman.ro/

The National Museum of the Romanian Peasant has a collection of textiles, icons, ceramics, and other artifacts of Romanian peasant life. One of Europe's leading museums of popular arts and traditions, it was designated "European Museum of the Year" in 1996.

☐ 33. Amzei Market

The Amzei Market is the main fresh market in Bucharest. Open from dawn until dusk, you will find a wide selection of fresh fruit and vegetables, fish, dairy products, breads, cakes, meats, flowers and garden plants. There are even live chickens! The open air stalls, many with colorful umbrellas offer the freshest ingredients.

☐ 34. History Museum of the Romanian Jews

Address: Strada Mămulari 3, Bucharest, Romania
Phone: 021/311.08.70
Web: http://romanianjewish.org/ro

The Jewish Museum in Bucharest is located in the former Templul Unirea Sfântă synagogue, which survived the Second World War. The museum opened in 2002 and is housed in a partially refurbished historic building designed by architect Alexander Pilski (1868-1943) and completed in 1906 under the auspices of the Romanian Orthodox Metropolitan Nifon Batorești.

☐ 35. Church of Bucur the Shepherd

Address: Splaiul Unirii, Bucharest, Romania
Web: http://www.biserica-bucur.ro/

On Calea Victoriei, the street that divides the Old City from both the Palace and the Rome quarter, a portal of white stone stands between two storey red brick houses. A prayer room with all its icons in it can be found inside one of Rome's oldest churches, dedicated to Saint Constantin 'Bucur' in Romanian. Built in 1743 following a fire in a former wooden church, this is one of the few churches that weren't demolished during Ceaușescu's rule in the 1980s.

☐ 36. Odeon Theatre

Address: Calea Victoriei 40-42, Bucharest, Romania
Phone: + 40 21 314 7234

Email: odeon.art@teatrul-odeon.ro
Web: http://www.teatrul-odeon.ro/eng/acasa.html

In 2005, the enterprise was inherited by the National Theatre from the Romanian National Opera, together with Teatrul Odeon and Teatrul Național din București. The Sala Odeon is a performance hall for various shows and events, that can accommodate 1,706 seated persons. The place hosts many other events as well, such as exhibitions, conferences and banquets.

☐ 37. "Theodor Pallady" Museum

Address: Strada Spătarului 22, Bucharest, Romania
Phone: 021/211.49.79

Email: national.art@art.museum.ro

Web: http://www.mnar.arts.ro/

The Theodor Pallady Museum is located in one of the oldest surviving merchant houses in Bucharest. Built between 1770 and 1773 and one of the most beautiful buildings situated on Calea Victoriei, it also hosts a number of remarkable paintings by Theodor Pallady. This museum includes some European and Oriental furniture pieces as well as precious objects from the 18th century.

☐ 38. Art Collections Museum

Address: Calea Victoriei 111, Bucharest, Romania

Phone: 021/211.17.49; 021/212.96.41

Email: national.art@art.museum.ro

Web: http://www.mnar.arts.ro/

The Art Collections Museum is housed in a monumental 18th century building that was donated to the museum by Prince Barbu Stirbei in 1907. The collections of this museum gather some art masterpieces of the 19th and 20th centuries (including, paintings, antiques and sculptures) from various European artists.

☐ 39. Kid's Town

Kid's Town, located in downtown Bucharest, has been a source of joy and happiness for children since 1990. In 1999, this amusement park was declared a natural monument by the Government of Bucharest City Hall. It is made up of five rides that have been preserved from the time of King Carol I of Romania's reign from 1866-1914. The rides display their safety certificates.

☐ 40. National Opera House Museum

Address: Bulevardul Mihail Kogălniceanu 70, Bucharest, Romania
Phone: 021/314.69.80

Witness the national pride and creative artistry embodied in the National Opera House, Bucharest. Standing as a cultural centerpiece of Romania, it is no surprise that this historic opera house attracts visitors from across the globe. Portraying the nation's rich history through its distinct architecture, theatergoers are treated to world-class performances on-stage—from classic Italian operas to modern American films.

☐ 41. Bulevardul Unirii

The Bulevardul Unirii was the most important modern road built in Romania between 1966 and 1979 under the rule of dictator Nicolae Ceauşescu. It crosses central Bucharest from north to south, connecting by bridges or tunnels important city areas such as Piaţa Universităţii (University Square), Piaţa Romana (Roman Square), Piaţa Unirii (Union Square) and Piaţa Presei Libere (Freedom of the Press Square).

☐ 42. Tăndărică Puppet Theatre

Address: Strada General Eremia Grigorescu 24, Bucharest, Romania
Phone: + 40 21 315 2377
Email: contact@teatrultandarica.ro
Web: http://en.teatrultandarica.ro/

The Tăndărică Puppet Theatre, Bucharest is a treasure. A puppet tradition for over 400 years here, the puppeteers wear traditional Romanian clothing and tell fabulous tales through their beautiful, brightly colored puppets that move as though they are alive. All shows begin with a warm up—watch as the storytellers present music, dance and mime.

☐ 43. Church of the Icon

Address: Strada Icoanei 12, Bucharest, Romania

One of the better-known churches in Bucharest is the Icoana, located on Piața Romană. The church was built by Mihail Băbeanu, Romanian secretary to Prince Vasile Lupu Nahache, between 1745 and 1750. The original name was Schitul Icoana ("Icon Hermitage") since it was intended as a small monastery. The construction lasted for six years and Mihail Băbeanu put his whole life into this building project, investing about half of his fortune.

Picture Credits

Bucharest, Romania Cover: Eu-eugen / 3125298 (Pixabay)
Stavropoleos Church: Andrei Stroe (CC BY 3.0)

Romanian Athenaeum: Mihai Petre (CC BY-SA 3.0 ro)
The Old Court/Princely Palace: Bogdan Caraman (CC BY-SA 3.0 ro)
Antim Monastery: Ştefan Jurcă (CC BY 2.0)
Saint Spyridon the New Church: Andrei Stroe (CC BY-SA 3.0 ro)
Calea Victoriei: Joe Mabel (CC-BY-SA-3.0)
University Square: Cristian Chirita (GFDL)
Palace of the National Military Circle: Jesús Gorriti (CC BY-SA 2.0)
Lipscani Street: Carpathianland (CC BY-SA 2.0)
Kretzulescu Church: Joe Mabel (CC-BY-SA-3.0)
National History Museum of Romania: Alexandra Hegedus (CC BY-SA 3.0 ro)
National Museum of Art of Romania: Nicubunu (CC BY-SA 3.0)
Armenian Church: Korinna (CC BY-SA 3.0 ro)
Dimitrie Gusti National Village Museum: Nicubunu (CC BY-SA 3.0 ro)
Carol Park: Daria Virbanescu (CC BY-SA 3.0 ro)
Youth's Park: Mihai Petre (CC BY-SA 3.0)
Unirea Shopping Center: Gabinho (CC BY 3.0)
Capitoline Wolf of Bucharest: Britchi Mirela (CC BY-SA 3.0 ro)
Prince Radu Vodă Monastery: Fusion-Of-Horizons (CC BY 2.0)
Royal Palace: Nicubunu (CC BY-SA 3.0)
Cotroceni Palace: Bekuletz (CC BY-SA 2.5)
Lake Cişmigiu: Calinos (CC BY-SA 3.0 ro)
Herăstrău Park: Crislia (CC BY-SA 4.0)
University Library: Jorge Láscar (CC BY 2.0)
Old Princely Court Church: Jorge Láscar (CC BY 2.0)
"I.L. Caragiale" National Theatre Museum: Julienbzh35 (CC BY-SA 3.0)
Bucureşti Mall: Dan69En (CC BY 2.5)
Stavropoleos Monastery: Fusion-Of-Horizons (CC BY 2.0)
National Museum of the Romanian Peasant: Joe Mabel (CC-BY-SA-

3.0)
Amzei Market: Joe Mabel (CC-BY-SA-3.0)
History Museum of the Romanian Jews: Joe Mabel (CC-BY-SA-3.0)
Church of Bucur the Shepherd: Fusion-Of-Horizons (CC BY 2.0)
Odeon Theatre: Bogdan Giușcă (CC BY 2.5)
Art Collections Museum: Sabin Iacob (CC BY-SA 2.0)

Printed in Great Britain
by Amazon